TEARS FOR MY ANCESTORS

By Malik Canty

aka WORD BIRD

TEARS FOR MY ANCESTORS
Copyright © 2014 Malik Canty

ISBN-13: 978-0692277461
ISBN-10: 0692277463

Inspired 4 U Publications

Published by Inspired 4 U Publications,
an imprint of Inspired 4 U Ministries, LLC

http://inspired4upublications.com

Published September 2014
Updated October 2019

FORWARD

I am so honored to have been chosen to take this journey and to witness the evolution of Malik Canty- now known as the eminent Word Bird. Early in his life, I was privileged to watch his poetic growth. I knew he had a gift and that success was down the road. James Allen wrote, *"Your vision is the promise of what you shall one day be; your ideal is the prophecy of what you shall at last unveil."*

Exploring the inner part of your consciousness is what this poet is about. Malik incorporates creative ideas inspired by the Universe, and he challenges the readers to reflect on history and life with truth as a guide. "Tears For My Ancestors" is another gem that is filled with an unsparing style of truth.

Get ready for a steady diet of words that should inspire you to honor and never forget those who didn't make it, and those whom others keep telling us to forget.

Everlasting,

Gwendolyn Gillis Grinnage
Spiritual Mother

CONTENTS

Forward

Author's Note   i

1   Weeping in the Waters   Pg. 1

2   The Calling   Pg. 2

3   Heavy Waters   Pg. 3

4   Across The Waters   Pg. 5

5   African Dungeons   Pg. 7

6   Mother Africa   Pg. 11

7   Middle Passage   Pg. 13

8   Our Ancestors   Pg. 15

9   Ebony: The Daughters' of Mother Earth   Pg. 17

10 Can You Imagine?   Pg. 19

11 Out of Africa   Pg. 21

12 Chocolate People   Pg. 23

13 African Roots   Pg. 25

14 Noose on the Loose   Pg. 27

15 Sacred Burial Grounds   Pg. 29

16 Dry Bones   Pg. 31

17 Never Healed   Pg. 33

18 Hidden Manuscripts   Pg. 35

19 Black Wave   Pg. 37

20 The MAAFA Stories   Pg. 39

21 Blood in the Sand   Pg. 41

22 Ancestral Tribute   Pg. 43

About The Author   Pg. 45

NOTE: *Tears For My Ancestors* was a finalist for the 2015 Phillis Wheatley Book Award in the Poetry Category. (QBR/Harlem Book Fair)

AUTHOR'S NOTE

Restless spirits of antiquity invade the privacy of my soul with messages that the living must acknowledge in order for them to find eternal peace. These few poetic notes were not written to entertain...

"Tears For My Ancestors" is a collection of works with a poetic flavor that seeks to re-tell the stories of a resilient people. I seek to remind readers of the strength, courage, and unyielding spirit of Black People ... I seek to make the readers think about the hidden manuscripts, slave ships, and dungeons that our people survived.

From the past to the future, these notes were written in tears because of all the untold stories that have been purposely omitted from the history books.

When I heard some of our misguided youth state, "I don't want to learn about no Africa," it brought tears to my eyes and sadness to my soul...

I am compelled to tell the stories of my Ancestors.

Malik "Word Bird" Canty

"Our cultural roots are the most ancient in the world. The spiritual concepts of our Ancestors gave birth to religious thought African people believe in the oneness of the African family through sacred time, which unites the past, the present and the future. Our Ancestors live with us."

— Marimba Ani

WEEPING IN THE WATERS

My
>   Soul
>   Heard
>   Weeping in the Waters.

My
>   Eyes

Saw the earth open and swallow all its grief into the sea…

>   Dreaming on the Wings of Revelation.

Judas didn't mean it, Cain didn't either…

>   Oh mankind, why must you continue to dine in the fires of
>   chaos?

THE CALLING

Out of the Silence, my Ancestors call to me…

The Voices of many torment my soul until I respond to them…

Ancestral Grief won't allow me to sleep in Peace.

Their stories – with all the antiquity of the Alpha and Omega – Must Be Told…

Their wasted blood – that has saturated the Earth – keeps their spirits in mourning.

The injustice that many of them received as flesh beings has kept Mother-Earth from being balanced…

Their Stories Must Be Told!

The Messages that I have been receiving in my soul must be unleashed so that my Ancestors can find rest and peace…

I No Longer Pretend Not To Hear Them.

HEAVY WATERS

Restless Spirits of Antiquity invade the privacy of my soul with messages that the living must acknowledge in order for them to find Peace...

Flashbacks of my Ancestors, who were burned, castrated, diabolically devastated, remind me over and over again to Tell Their Stories!

When I pass any tree, the roots call out to me because the lynching of so many of my Ancestors are embedded in the Soul of the Trees.

Heavy Waters...

Dripping with agonizing memories that have managed to sustain themselves for centuries...

Waiting for a human vessel to deliver the painstaking horrors that others keep telling us to forget.

From the crevice of my soul, the words seek to surface...

The oceans, the rivers, and all those watery graveyards, every now and then, will exhale and release their fury to the surface.

Heavy waters...

When I hear the Youth of Today say, "I don't want to learn about no Africa," it brings tears to my eyes because *ignorance* of history can lead to a repeat of history.

Heavy Waters...

Heritage denial keeps the ancestors stirring in their graves because not all of them were slaves or enslaved.

Tell their stories… Tell their stories… Justice and reparations have also been found lost and drowning in the waters…

Open your mind as well as your eyes, seek truth because there is always proof.

How will the Children of Tomorrow learn if the adults keep swimming in the waters of denial?

Take time for truth, the children are waiting to follow your lead…

Heavy Waters …

Not made for swimming…

Not made for the weak, and not made for those who mate with deceit.

ACROSS THE WATERS

I am my Brothers' keeper.

The shadow has been cast, our view of each other has been orchestrated...

To keep us from finding the bloodlines that were separated and devastated on those deadly ancient ships, carrying our ancestors,

Across the Waters...

Into a new reality of "Servitude for Life" for all non-whites...

Across the waters...

By the millions, our people came bound in chains.

Across the Waters...

Into a triangle, where sharks and other sea creatures feasted until they filled their bellies...

Across the Waters...

Kings... Queens... Tribal... Nomadic... Villages... Kingdoms...

Across the Waters...

Black faces... Brown faces... Beautiful faces... Determined faces... Angry faces... Brutalized faces.

Across the Waters...

The presence of our lost ancestors often rides the waves to remind the living that there will be no forgiving or forgetting of the kidnapping and the brutality done to the flesh, on those ships and in those dungeons.

Across the Waters...

New world... Scattered tribes... Re-Creation and Separation of an ancient people from each other, from their culture, from their Gods and Goddesses...

Across the Waters...

Still strong... Still unyielding... Still defiant...

I Am my Brothers' keeper, even though he knows me not...

Across the Waters...

When the blood calls, will you recognize your kin?

Here I stand, a representative of a lost Tribe.

Across the Waters....

Zulu, Yoruba, Ashanti, Mali, Known and Unknown tribes, all chained and dragged to the turbulent waters, by hands that didn't give-a-damn about a Black Man, Woman or Child...

Across the Waters...

AFRICAN DUNGEONS

Through the eyes of a poet, I will mentally take you back into a time period of unspeakable horror for the people of African descent...

The African Dungeons, which were sometimes called Castles, were erected as Temples for the ungodly to Torture, Mutilate, and Break the Will of a Resilient and Proud People...

Surrounded by coastal waters, which were used as a graveyard for the defiant and those not strong enough to make the journey...

A graveyard for those who jumped overboard into the waiting mouth of a shark or other sea creatures that followed the ships.

The African Dungeons were filled with corridors that led to Doorways of No Return...

If the Walls and Floors could speak, it would drive a chill throughout your body and you would begin to understand why our children should be told these stories, even if it's too gory.

Huddled by the hundreds in thick chains that bound every part of their bodies...

They were crunched and bunched like wild beasts that had No rights and no words that could stop or slow down the beatings and mistreatments toward their flesh.

Chains bound the wounded, the sick, the defiant, the dead, and the children, into one link of around-the-clock agony...

Screams bounce off the walls, penetrating nothing...

Dark, dank, sweltering heat and rats feasting on the weak...

One Cube Window; the smell of death filled the air and made breathing almost impossible...

Guarded by men with guns, whose mission was devil led...

Whose hands enjoyed the pools of blood they created, while waiting to lead the survivors into the "coffin" of profit ships.

The African Dungeons, a place where today's history books have purposely omitted the atrocities that took place for over five hundred years...

Hidden history, kept from public view, purposely held back so that accountability is not served in the future to those who seek justice and reparations.

Sanctioned by those who prayed and tried to make God and accomplice to their alleged Natural Rights to Rule while on Earth...

Lies were nurtured and given validity so that generations would remain perpetually protected from the Sins of their Fathers.

Our children have a right to know and those of you who know some truth, studied some truth, must spread that truth...

It's time for the Lies to die because the African Roots did Survive...

Teach the children...

Our future depends on the generation that opens their eyes and hears the cries of the Ancestors, known and unknown...

Teach the children...

I can still hear the whips and see the ships
that took your children away.

MOTHER AFRICA

The sounds of the drums could be heard in every village with talks of strangers landing on the shores of Mother Africa, bearing strange gifts in exchange for warriors defeated in tribal wars...

"We will take them back with us," said the strangers, back to our world and make them work."

This was the beginning of slavery and the destruction of Black Culture...

Back and forth came the cargo ships in search of free labor to build the new world.

Back and Forth...

Every man, woman, child was in danger because of the new strangers who spoke with a devilish charm...

Loading and reloading their ships to capacity with human cargo.

The screams of Mother Africa were piercing, as village after village was decimated to the point of non-existence...

The clanging of chains could be heard, mixed in with the screams of the people, who were being led to the ships.

Former kings and queens dethroned in their own home...

Chains on their ankles, around their hands, necks, binding the various tribes together.

The bleeding of Mother Africa started off subtle and then it came out in gushes, turning the continent upside down…

All the richness, greatness, antiquity came tumbling down.

A Voyage of Death…

Back and forth, they came with their chains…

They decimated, planned on annihilating, the whole continent of Africa.

Mother Africa, I have heard you weeping in my soul for the countless generations of children that you have lost.

I can still hear the whips and see the ships that took your children away…

Gather your children Mother Africa wherever they might be, because it's the only way you will find peace and the only way to stop being damaged by the followers of the beast.

MIDDLE PASSAGE

The ships were always dark and dank, filled with a stench that was offensive to the nose and soul...

Screams were considered normal to the crew of men who only saw profit, not people...

Thick chains, guns, brutal force were tools used to beat the Africans into total submission.

The smell of death seeped out from the bowels of the ships and mingled with a repugnant odor that reeked with the abuse of those stacked below the decks like dying fish.

Festering wounds, maggot buffet, lined up, stacked up, hooked fish waiting to be gutted .

Forced feedings, rapes and beatings of men and women, who tried to resist their captivity .

Jumping overboard with children in arms, in bellies, was an act of honor instead of trying to survive those slave ship horrors.

Clanging heavy chains that bound necks, feet, hands, could be seen and heard on every African, didn't matter the age, size, or gender.

Middle Passage...

Where sharks feasted on those who were thrown overboard because of excess or defiance...

Thrown overboard because of sickness or an inability to withstand dreadful conditions.

Middle Passage...

A Fatal Journey...

The history books will never be able to tell the actual and factual number of those who did not survive those deadly voyages.

Middle Passage...

Where Africans became human cargo, forcefully transported across the Atlantic to be enslaved...

Brutality was the only reality on those deadly ships.

Middle Passage...

We should never forget the atrocities that befell the children of Mother Africa.

Middle Passage...

The waters still weep.

OUR ANCESTORS

The Ocean ran Red with the Dead... One Hundred Million Bodies...

Your Ancestors, My Ancestors, Our Ancestors...

The screams from the depths of the ocean floors became silent only because of the perseverance of the Survivors.

Your Ancestors, My Ancestors, Our Ancestors...

How could we allow ourselves to ever forget those who never made it into the Record Books and remain nameless as if they never ever existed?

The strangers came in ships to conquer and to stock-up on Human Cargo to help build their world...

Cramped quarters, death boxes, and piles of flesh squeezed together for a Middle Passage ride to a New Way of Life for those who were not White.

Your Ancestors, My Ancestors, , Our Ancestors...

No one enjoyed this fatal journey more than the Sharks...

Man Overboard! Woman Overboard! Nation Overboard!

The Bermuda Triangle and its mysteries, only exist because of the restless spirits who still yearn for Justice, for Payback!

Your Ancestors, My Ancestors, Our Ancestors...

I Am Here to Collect a Debt.

They saw in you a strength that was found only in men,
yet a tenderness that only a Goddess could possess.

EBONY: THE DAUGHTERS
OF MOTHER EARTH

It started on those Terror Ships...

They couldn't wait to get their bloody, murderous hands on you...

To take you in their arms by force and debase, disgrace, and rape you...

They wanted to taste your Forbidden Fruits because you have always been more than just cute.

They wanted to capture your Unyielding Spirit through the abuse and misuse of your bodies...

They saw in you a strength that was found only in men, yet a tenderness that only a Goddess could possess...

They thought by mating with you, they could own you mentally and physically...

You were always their Favorite Nighttime Desert.

When the babies started dropping, they disowned you and your children, but never kept their hands off you...

They shackled your bodies and took you *against your will* so many times, but they could never kill your Unyielding Spirit.

Ebony: Your Mind has been the source of your strength since the beginning...

Ebony: You are the Daughters of Mother Earth.

Many have trampled on you, hurt you, and denied you the majestic riches you deserve, but they could never, ever, take your soul from you...

Many have sought to claim you, train you, some even boast they have tamed you...

Remember, Royalty is in your DNA...

Beauty, as well as strength, is in your DNA...

Your Divine Natural Aura enriched the Earth and created the First Birth.

Ebony, dry those eyes, you were not born to cry; it's time for you to RISE...

CAN YOU IMAGINE?

Human Cargo...

Flesh Chains thrown overboard because of excess...

Watery Graveyard...

Disregard for Black Life.

Sunken Black Treasures Buried All Along the Coast...

Bermuda Triangle...

Screams coming from below and above the waters... Man, Woman, Child, Shark Food...

Agony... Torture... Mass Hysteria...

Can you imagine the fear they must have felt not knowing where they were going or why?

Can you imagine not understanding the language of those who captured you?

Can you imagine the terror they must have felt, the hopelessness, as they were bound with heavy chains from head to feet?

Can you imagine the anger the men must have felt watching the Beast have its way with their women?

Can you imagine seeing your mother or your brothers and sisters torn from your arms and thrown overboard into the abyss of the waters?

Can you imagine your ancestors, some of whom were Kings and Queens, huddled in the bottom of the ship, frightened and stacked like logs on top of each other; urinating on each other; releasing their waste on each other, smothering and dying in each other's arms?

Some people, for whatever reasons, don't want us to remember these events that actually happened, to your ancestors, my ancestors, our ancestors…

How can we ever forget when their pain has transcended space and time to remind us of the atrocities that befell them?

Can you imagine?

I Can!

OUT OF AFRICA

It's been called the Dark Continent by those who sought to implant lies and half-truths about this magnificent place...

So many people were brainwashed to believe the Tarzan stories, and they mocked and ridiculed the men and women of this continent...

So many Invaders polluted and raped the land and people, then spread vicious rumors of savages and cannibals, who had to be enslaved, who had no valuable culture, and no history worth mentioning ...

So many foreign scholars came and saw the beauty, antiquity, and still reported lies about the splendor of this Ancient Place.

Out of Africa came the First Man and Woman to walk the earth and start civilization on its path...

Out of Africa, Great Civilizations rose and migrated to every part of the world, bringing their knowledge and skills with them...

Mali... Timbuktu... Egypt... Kush... Sudan... Songhay, set precedence that are still relevant today.

Out of Africa came the Garden of Eden...

The Cradle of Civilization began here on the Dark Continent...

The Pyramids, the Great Sphinx, and Totem Poles that revealed hidden symbolic messages of the greatness of the people and land came Out of Africa...

Genetic Material, giving undeniable proof that Africa is the Birth Place of Civilization, has always been available to those who seek truth...

Out of Africa came Mansa-Musa, Shaka Zulu, Jomo Kenyatta, Steven Biko, Patrice Lumumba, Winnie and Nelson Mandela, _____, _____, _____ the list is long and strong...

Out of Africa came the Spirit of Life that traveled and grew to every part of the earth.

It's time to get that denial out of your mind and pay homage...

Out of Africa came the Soul of Man and the Beginning of Man.

CHOCOLATE PEOPLE

Rich in Flavor, made to do the labor of all Nations...

Chocolate People...

Your Blood is Sacred... Your Strength is Unmatched...

The World was once under Your Rule.

Chocolate People...

Survivors of Slave Ships, Murder, Rape and Torture...

Survivors of Jim Crow Laws and dehumanizing treatment towards your minds and bodies...

You were turned inside out, given new names such as Nig@*r, Coon, Worthless, Undependable, Childlike, and told you were created for servitude.

Chocolate People... Original People... the First people who walked the planet, easily duped because of your natural trust and loving nature...

Pyramid Builders... Pharaohs... Star-Gazers...

Those Black Hands that others despise has helped Shaped this World...

That Strong, Ancient, Black Mind has instilled in it the Keys of Life.

Chocolate People...

Be Proud of Your Color for you are like no others...

Rich like the Nile River, there has never been a tribe called Nig@*rs.

The Ancestors are patiently waiting for your return to the Throne of Your Mind...

AFRICAN ROOTS

Children of the African Roots where is the love you should have for each other? Where is the love?

Have you no shame mocking each other's culture, or do you really believe you are different from one another?

Children of the African Roots scattered on different islands throughout the world: Jamaica, Puerto Rico, Santa Domingo, Guyana, Trinidad, just to name a few.

The only difference in each of you is the culture you are accustomed to.

The Roots of your history comes from the shores of Mother Africa.

When I hear you down each other, have disdain for each other, taunt and make mockery of each other's ways and customs, my soul weeps.

Children of the African Roots Heritage, denial has kept you divided.

Instead of embracing each other, you are leery of one another.

Diabolical planning that was set in motion centuries ago has kept your hands around each other's throat.

Until the veil of ignorance is removed from your eyes, many of you will never realize that you All are Children of the African Roots...

Love each other for you can't make it without one another.

Waiting for another opportunity... another place to hang with menacing pride and put to rest the Lie that Racism has Died.

NOOSE ON THE LOOSE

Noose on the loose...

Last seen hanging around an institution, upsetting faculty and students of all nationalities...

Stirring memories of Night Riders, who brought Fear and Death whenever the Noose appeared.

Noose on the loose...

Trying to outdo the wicked hands that will draw a swastika on a building, on a house, and on a Temple, to make its evil presence felt.

Saw it in the South, the North, and the West...

Saw it in the eyes of the elders, who still remember Jim Crow, Willie Lynch, and all those laws that regulated their humanity...

It openly revealed itself in JENA and one of God's trees had to pay for it.

Noose on the loose...

Enemy of every tree that carries in its roots the screams of an Ancestor, a stranger, or someone who would not conform to a sick norm.

Noose on the loose...

Teach the children about the history and the reality of what hate symbols truly mean and who they are meant for.

Noose on the loose…

Waiting for another opportunity, another place, to hang with menacing pride and put to rest the Lie that Racism has Died…

Open your eyes… Evil is on the Rise!

Noose still on the loose.

SACRED BURIAL GROUNDS

The Bones kept appearing from beneath the surface, showing themselves in fragments...

A leg bone here, an arm bone there, pieces of a hidden history everywhere.

A lost part of a nation within this nation ...

Separated from its past, unknown to the descendants of its future.

Old Dry Bones stirring in their graves, not all of them were slaves.

The History books have to be changed in order to stop their pain and tell their stories.

This Burial Ground has now become Holy Grounds, these spirits yearn to be free and seek their true place in history.

We, as their descendants, must somehow pay Homage to their spirits...

We must have them included, not secluded from the rest of antiquity...

We should honor them, even if we don't know much about them...

We should build a memorial and revise the history books; the spirits have once again spoken...

A leg bone here, an arm bone there, pieces of a forgotten history everywhere.

Buried history rising up out the dirt, seeking rest and seeking respect...

A leg bone here, an arm bone there, forgotten history is buried everywhere.

DRY BONES

Dry Bones…

The voices of many coming from the Waters…

A New Day being controlled by an Old Way…

Sleep Time of the Mind is on Overtime…

Check out the shores of mankind; Satan Lives.

Go to Rwanda, Zaire, and Ethiopia, where starvation and devastation have taken up residence…

Indifference, Coldness, in the Hearts of Many…

Who weeps for the desolate?

Pandora's Box…

Who picked the lock?

Aids, Ebola, and Crack, somehow the words Biological and Diabolical warfare seem to be attached…

The Murders are still going on.

Satan is no longer in the minds of some, he has replaced their Heart with his Cold Heart.

Look around with a true clear vision, can you not see the misery, so close, so close, that you can almost taste the despair that is out there…

The murderous heart that has set tribe against tribe, man against woman, and children against parents, is smiling at his work because his mission is to turn the world upside down.

Dry Bones can't find home and can't find God when He is everywhere...

Descendants of Pyramid Builders are now homeless; the Spirits of Antiquity will remain dormant no longer because evil is getting stronger...

We must find a way to get God back into the classrooms, back into the ever changing heart of men and women.

Old Dry Bones...

Stirring...

Restless in their resting place...

Can't find home...

Can't find God when He is everywhere!

NEVER HEALED

The wounds have never healed...

The recurring nightmares and residue of slavery now haunts our children...

Haunts them in ways that manifest itself in their frustration and anger...

Haunts them where many of them don't care to hear about history... Don't care to hear about loving themselves above all else.

The wounds have never healed...

Slave mentality still a reality for many of the descendants of Africa...

Scattered seeds ... The Great African Tree continues to bleed for her lost children, who have been taught and conditioned to forget Her...

Our fears have not disappeared.

The MAAFA stories must continue to be told for generations to come...

The stories of Colonization... Enslavement... Castration of Black Men... Jim Crow and his legion... Rape of our women... Displacement of the black families... Willie Lynch and the White House Pimps... must be told.

Our Wounds have Not Healed.

We must face the present with energy, vigor, and teach our children to stop calling themselves Nig@**s...

Teach the children so that generation after generation rediscovers that the strength of black people is like no other...

The strength of Black People will always surface during our darkest hour.

Scattered Seeds of Antiquity... Survivors of a Black Holocaust... your indomitable Spirit could never be broken.

Our Wounds have Not Healed...

Our Tears have Not Stopped... Justice has not come to folks who need it... Racism is still running amuck and setting up shop in the Big White House...

Lost children of the Great African Tree, as long as you remain apart from each other, disrespect each other, not see the Imago-Dei in each other...

Our Wounds Will Never Heal!

HIDDEN MANUSCRIPTS

They burned the most important books, replaced and remade others with lies and half-truths, all done with precision to make sure you were great no more...

Generations had to be fooled, truth had to be diluted, and other magnificent cultures had to be reduced to Myths.

The Hiding of certain Manuscripts was an elaborate plan designed to enslave certain sects of humanity...

Designed by those who would conquer and control others that have been deemed weak and uncivilized...

The Hidden Manuscripts hold the truth and proof of Great Civilizations that did exist, no matter what their descendants are going through today.

So many books were burned, altered pages, words added and others removed, to ensure that the lies that were said, would spread...

New books replaced old books and told of people who had no direction, no culture worth mentioning, no history that is important, and no contributors to the growth of mankind...

The Hidden Manuscripts and their contents have kept many people from finding out that their Race is Great.

Take away a people's History and you take away their Soul...

So many books were burned while other were stored in secret vaults and private collections...

Others have been released and tampered with false ideology.

Our children are disillusioned because of our inability to find and teach the Hidden Manuscripts to them...

Begin a search...

Wake Up and Read the Right Books...

Truth lies in the Readers, who are no longer followers of the great deceivers.

BLACK WAVE

There was a scream coming from the bottom of the Ocean Floor, causing the Sea and other Bodies of Water to Rise...

Watery graveyards, containing the remnant of ships and people whose spirits have been exiled to the waters...

Sunken treasures disguised as African people were buried at sea before their time, making the Black Wave Rise.

Building momentum on the wings of patience, a Black Wave is coming...

Washing away centuries of mistreatment, staking claim on being the first inhabitants of this planet.

A Black Wave will frighten and enlighten many because it's been coming for quite some time...

It had been contained by racism, trapped and altered by slavery, yet it still keeps coming...

A Black Wave will make this planet shake for it means that the original Black man is finally starting to awake!

You may curse me under your breath, mock and scorn me; still, you won't stop me for I am part of a Black Wave...

You can tangle with me over Civil Rights and Affirmative Action Programs; but still, you won't stop me.

Look for signs of me in the near future because I-Am-Coming, bringing the spirit and aspirations of my ancestors with me...

Check out the Shores of Mankind...

A   Black   Wave   is   Coming...

Racism can't stop it, descendants of Jim Crow can't stop it...

Watch for the signs.

THE MAAFA STORIES

Millions upon Millions of our Ancestors did not survive the Horror of the Middle Passage.

Slave Ships... Whips... Mass murders... Torture... Rape of women and men...

The MAAFA stories must be told to all generations.

The coastal waters are a graveyard filled with black people...

The overstuffed bellies of sharks and other sea creatures that feasted on the bodies of our Ancestors must be told...

The wicked, vicious, inhumane behavior by the oppressors who came to Mother Africa to steal the wealth of that rich continent must be told...

The Blood, the Royal and common blood, of tribe after tribe of African people that kept the ocean floor red must be told!

The spirit of those lost lives still dwell under the ocean floor...

We must set them free and tell the truth, no matter who gets upset, their spirits must find rest...

Do you hear the drums?

No lie can live forever ...

History must be told as it truly happened...

Do you hear the Drums?

Coming from the bottom of the ocean floor as truth begins to march into the consciousness of the world…

The MAAFA stories with all their brutality is a reality for people of African descent, of Native American descent.

We weep for the slaughter of others, we understand them and we stand with them in their remembrance… Still…

Millions upon millions of black people lost their lives unjustly…

Millions upon millions are unknown and stories untold because of their early demise from the earth.

Will we ever know the actual number of deaths that took place on those fatal journeys through the Middle Passage?

Will we ever really know?

I don't think so.

BLOOD IN THE SAND

For years they would come to the waters... Clothed in white... Beaming under the night light... Seeking to communicate and remind the Ancestors that they have not been forgotten...

They would gather in the hundreds and the beach would become a Sacred Place to remind the living of the deaths that took place, of the Ancestors who were dragged and beaten upon their arrival to these shores.

Blood in the Sand...

The sand is filled with the DNA of the Ancestors who survived the horrors of the Middle Passage, the beatings and inhumane treatment of their flesh by their captors...

In the sand, the blood fell and the earth exhaled, making the waters roar while the rain came down like tears...

Every drop measured in the millions, mingling with the rain, blending with the tears and in harmony with the sacred dancing and music.

Blood in the Sand...

The waters could not cover up the atrocities done to those who made it to these shores...

Made it despite the rapes, torture, and brutality that was heaped upon them by those who refused to see them as human.

Blood in the Sand...

A reminder that the water was not the only graveyard for the captured Africans...

Every year, the lost fruit of the African roots would come to pay homage for the MAAFA Stories, show respect and make sure the World Never Forgets.

Blood in the Sand...

Untold stories seeking a way out...

Every drum beat is a heartbeat of a lost and stolen life.

Who will tell their stories?

ANCESTRAL TRIBUTE

This tribute is for my Ancestors, who are Unknown because they were omitted from the history books...

Unknown because they were snatched from the womb and cradle before they could grow...

Unknown because their rebellious spirits caused them an early demise on this planet by those who could not break or subdue their fighting spirits...

Unknown because they were thrown overboard or jumped overboard during the horrors of the Middle Passage.

This tribute is for my Ancestors, who worked the plantations from Sun-Up to Sun-Down with disgust and mistrust of anyone who tried to justify their enslavement...

No amendments can ever make up for some of the atrocities done to my people on those ships, in those dungeons, and on those plantations.

This is for the unsung voices that are buried in the murky waters of the Mississippi, in the backwoods of Alabama, on the bottom of the Ocean floors...

Time Has Not Let Their Spirits Rest.

This is a tribute for my Ancestors...

Join me in paying homage to those whose spirits are still living in the shadows, riding on the wind, restless because they will always be Unknown.

This tribute was written in anger, written in tears...

It is a reminder to those of us, who are here today and have no knowledge of yesterday...

The spirits of our Unknown live in all of us.

You Honor our Ancestors when you, take time to acknowledge them...

Join me in the realm of your heart, so that they can all be free.

ABOUT THE AUTHOR

Malik Canty is a Retired Educator, Spiritual Poet, and Author, who speaks for the voiceless. Known around the poetry circuit as the Word Bird, Malik has performed in various places such as, The Apollo Theatre, Brooklyn Academy of Music, The Shomburg Cultural Center, and at the McDonalds Gospelfest as a semi-finalist. He has also been published in several magazines, newsletters and anthologies; as well as been a featured Poet on 89.9 FM radio.

In addition, Malik "Word Bird" Canty is the author of "Who Hears the Poet When He Weeps?"; "Poetic Fire"; and 2 editions of "Words From The River," of which Rev. Dr. Johnny Ray Youngblood dubbed him "prophetic in his poetry" and "Poet Laureate" of St. Paul Community Baptist Church, in the book's introduction.

Word Bird writes to reveal the messages in his soul and as a witness of the durability of his people. The spirit and eyes of many speak to his soul, which leads him to intuitively write and speak for those individuals or groups who are afraid, incapable of expressing themselves, or don't know how to communicate effectively.

If Word Bird lands by you, there is a message for you. Let whosoever has an ear, hear and pay attention to what the spirits have to say. It is sure to be a "feeding time for the mind" experience.

For more information or to book Word Bird for an event, visit http://malikcanty.com. Have Words, Will Travel!